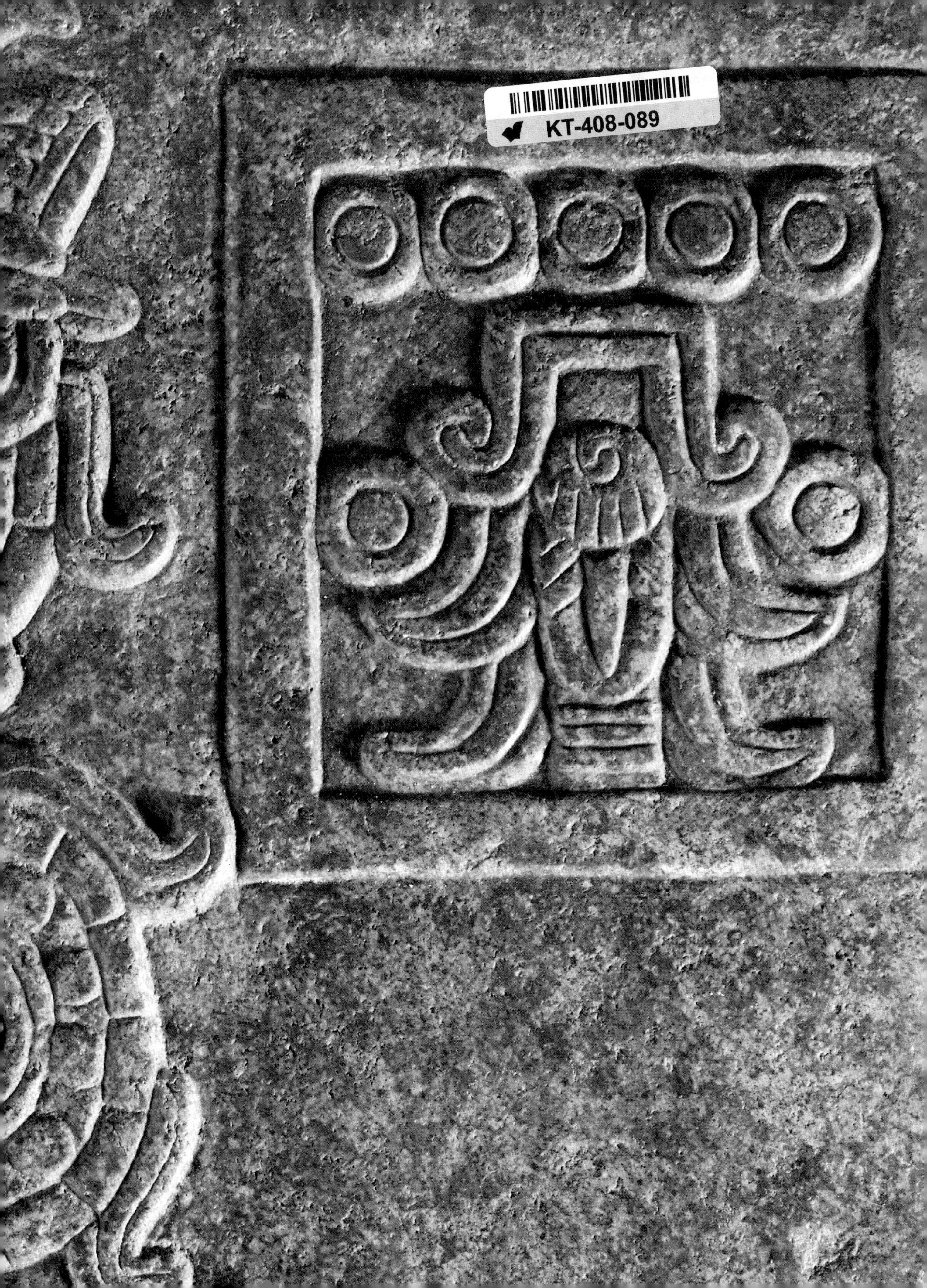

BRAITHWAITE C of E. SCHOOL

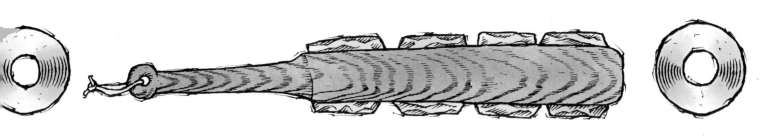

THE FACTS ABOUT

THE AZTECS

Jen Green

WAYLAND

First published in Great Britain in 1994 by Simon and Schuster Young Books
Reprinted by Macdonald Young Books in 1997 as *What Do
We Know About the Aztecs* by Joanna Defrates
This differentiated text edition by Jen Green,
published in 2007 by Wayland
Copyright © Wayland 2007

Wayland
338 Euston Road
London NW1 3BH

Wayland Australia
Level 17/207 Kent Street
Sydney, NSW 2000

Original series design: Dave West
Illustrator: Rob Shone
Layout for this edition: Jane Hawkins
Editor for this edition: Katie Powell

British Library Cataloguing in Publication Data
 Green, Jen
   Facts about the Aztecs
   1. Aztecs - Juvenile literature 2. Mexico - History
   - To
   1519 - Juvenile literature
   I. Title II. The Aztecs
   972'.018
ISBN 978 0 7502 5262 1

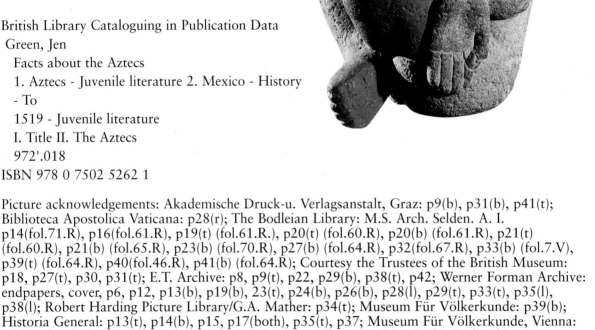

Picture acknowledgements: Akademische Druck-u. Verlagsanstalt, Graz: p9(b), p31(b), p41(t);
Biblioteca Apostolica Vaticana: p28(r); The Bodleian Library: M.S. Arch. Selden. A. I.
p14(fol.71.R), p16(fol.61.R), p19(t) (fol.61.R.), p20(t) (fol.60.R), p20(b) (fol.61.R), p21(t)
(fol.60.R), p21(b) (fol.65.R), p23(b) (fol.70.R), p27(b) (fol.64.R), p32(fol.67.R), p33(b) (fol.7.V),
p39(t) (fol.64.R), p40(fol.46.R), p41(b) (fol.64.R); Courtesy the Trustees of the British Museum:
p18, p27(t), p30, p31(t); E.T. Archive: p8, p9(t), p22, p29(b), p38(t), p42; Werner Forman Archive:
endpapers, cover, p6, p12, p13(b), p19(b), 23(t), p24(b), p26(b), p28(l), p29(t), p33(t), p35(l),
p38(l); Robert Harding Picture Library/G.A. Mather: p34(t); Museum Für Völkerkunde: p39(b);
Historia General: p13(t), p14(b), p15, p17(both), p35(t), p37; Museum Für Völkerkunde, Vienna:
p26(t); South American Pictures: p43(t); TRIP/Andrew Gasson: p25, p34(b), Richard Powers:
p43(b)

Every effort has been made to clear copyright. Should there be any inadvertent omission please
apply to the publisher for rectification.

Printed in China
Wayland is a division of Hachette Children's Books, a Hachette Livre UK Company.

Endpapers: This sculpture is from Tenochtitlan and shows the Feathered Serpent, the symbol
of the god Quetzalcoatl.

CONTENTS

Words that appear in **BOLD** can be found in the glossary on page 44.

WHO WERE THE AZTECS?

The Aztecs were a people who lived in the high plateau-land of central Mexico around AD 1400. Between 1345 and 1520, they ruled an empire that covered much of central Mexico. The Aztecs were fierce and warlike, but also skilled at crafts. They ruled from their city, Tenochtitlan.

◀ A WANDERING PEOPLE

The Aztecs had not always lived in central Mexico. They arrived in a high valley, called the Valley of Mexico, around AD 1200. Before that, they had been wandering for about two hundred years. The Aztecs believed their tribal god, Huitzilopochtli, protected them as they wandered. He also showed them where to settle and found a city by sending a sign. The sign was an eagle sitting on a cactus, eating a serpent.

◀ BUILDING AN EMPIRE

The Aztecs founded the city of Tenochtitlan in about AD 1325. As the city grew, the Aztecs traded with neighbouring people. Gradually they took over the surrounding lands to become the strongest people. By 1500 Tenochtitlan was the centre of a powerful empire. But twenty years later, the Aztecs were invaded and conquered by a Spanish army.

◀ AZTEC CAPITAL

Tenochtitlan was built on an island in Lake Texcoco. The city was divided into four districts. **Causeways** were built to connect the island to the shore.

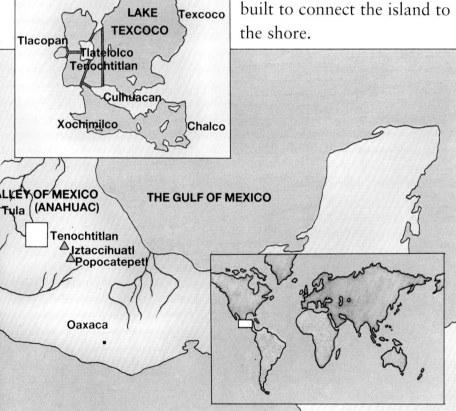

▲ HOW DO WE KNOW?

We know about the Aztecs by uncovering the remains of buildings they constructed. Experts called **archaeologists** uncover these remains. The Aztecs also made picture books called **Codices**. The Spanish destroyed many of these, but some survived. Pictures like the one above show scenes from Aztec life. The Spanish also wrote about Aztec customs.

TIMELINE	AD	1200	1250	1300	1350	1400
VALLEY OF MEXICO		Aztecs enter the valley from the north.	The valley is inhabited by several peoples who often fight one another. Aztecs settle near Lake Texcoco.	The city of Tenochtitlan is founded. Aztecs drain the swamps and build **causeways** and canals.	The priest-ruler Tenoch dies. The Aztecs are still ruled by a people called the Tepanecs, who control the valley.	The Tepanecs are defeated. The Aztecs expand their territory to rule the whole valley. Other peoples send them **tributes**.
EUROPE		Fourth Crusade. Magna Carta is signed.	The English kings gain power in Britain.	Battle of Bannockburn. Scotland defeats England.	Black Death in Europe is followed by economic collapse. Peasants Revolt in England.	England defeats France at the Battle of Agincourt. England gradually loses its land in France. Wars of the Roses in England.
ASIA AND AFRICA		Mongols under Genghis Khan begin to conquer Asia.	Marco Polo visits the court of Kublai Khan in China. Rise of the Ottoman Empire.	Europeans trade with Africa via the Middle East. Salt and luxury goods are exchanged for gold and slaves.	China under the Ming dynasty becomes a powerful state. It exports silk and cotton to the West.	Kingdom of Benin is set up in Africa. European explorers search for a sea-route to China and India via the Caribbean.
ARTS AND SCIENCES		Age of Gothic architecture. European cathedrals are built.	Age of great Italian poets, including Petrarch and Dante. Latin is the language of professionals in Europe. Islamic architecture reaches India.	Italians invent spectacles. The Kremlin is built in Moscow.	The Aztecs write the **Codices** and develop a complex calendar.	The Italian Renaissance begins. Fortress of Zimbabwe is built in Africa. The first book is printed in Europe.

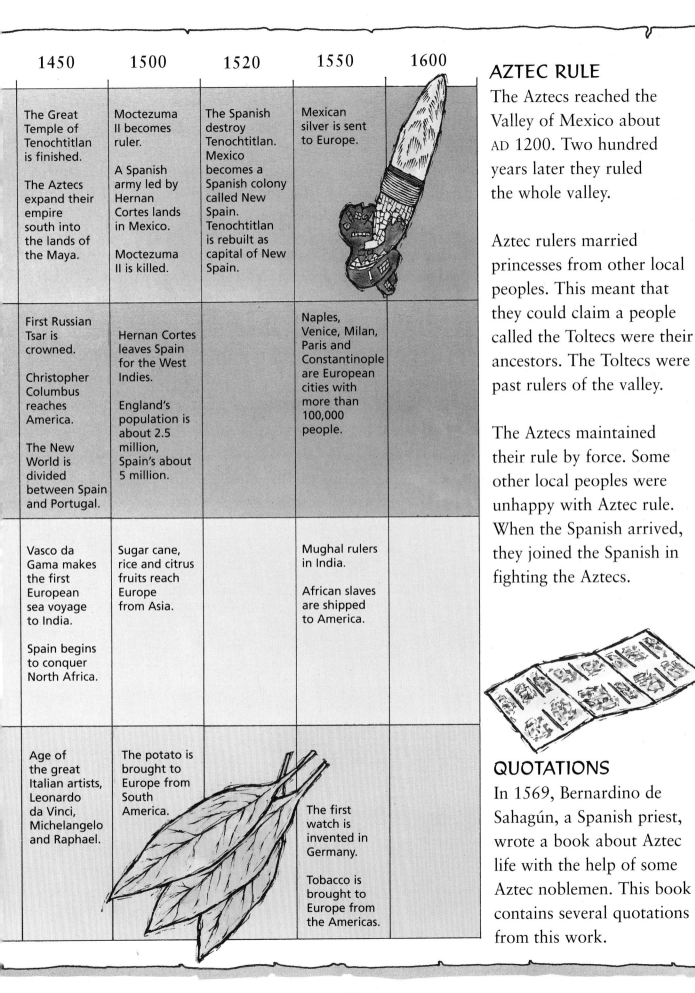

1450	1500	1520	1550	1600
The Great Temple of Tenochtitlan is finished. The Aztecs expand their empire south into the lands of the Maya.	Moctezuma II becomes ruler. A Spanish army led by Hernan Cortes lands in Mexico. Moctezuma II is killed.	The Spanish destroy Tenochtitlan. Mexico becomes a Spanish colony called New Spain. Tenochtitlan is rebuilt as capital of New Spain.	Mexican silver is sent to Europe.	
First Russian Tsar is crowned. Christopher Columbus reaches America. The New World is divided between Spain and Portugal.	Hernan Cortes leaves Spain for the West Indies. England's population is about 2.5 million, Spain's about 5 million.		Naples, Venice, Milan, Paris and Constantinople are European cities with more than 100,000 people.	
Vasco da Gama makes the first European sea voyage to India. Spain begins to conquer North Africa.	Sugar cane, rice and citrus fruits reach Europe from Asia.		Mughal rulers in India. African slaves are shipped to America.	
Age of the great Italian artists, Leonardo da Vinci, Michelangelo and Raphael.	The potato is brought to Europe from South America.		The first watch is invented in Germany. Tobacco is brought to Europe from the Americas.	

AZTEC RULE

The Aztecs reached the Valley of Mexico about AD 1200. Two hundred years later they ruled the whole valley.

Aztec rulers married princesses from other local peoples. This meant that they could claim a people called the Toltecs were their ancestors. The Toltecs were past rulers of the valley.

The Aztecs maintained their rule by force. Some other local peoples were unhappy with Aztec rule. When the Spanish arrived, they joined the Spanish in fighting the Aztecs.

QUOTATIONS

In 1569, Bernardino de Sahagún, a Spanish priest, wrote a book about Aztec life with the help of some Aztec noblemen. This book contains several quotations from this work.

HOW DID THE AZTECS FARM?

The Aztecs were successful farmers, even though the climate of central Mexico was harsh, and the land was not very fertile. The main crops were maize, beans and squashes. Around the city of Tenochtitlan, farmers grew crops in **chinampas**, or floating gardens. These gardens were built on land reclaimed from the shallow bed of the lake.

▼ FLOATING GARDENS

The floating gardens were built on the lake by piling rich mud from the lake bottom into a strong framework made of branches, and weighted down with stones. Farmers used a network of canals between the gardens to get about by boat.

THE FARMING YEAR

Aztec farmers had to work hard to feed the people of Tenochtitlan. The picture on the right shows hard-working and lazy farmers. The farming year was regulated to try to prevent famine. Days for planting, sowing, weeding and harvesting were all fixed by law.

▼ TOOLS

Aztec farmers used wooden hoes and digging sticks to turn the soil. The digging stick worked like a modern spade. The Aztecs had no ploughs, horses, or wheeled vehicles such as carts.

Digging stick

Hoe

▼ GOD OF THE MAIZE

People ate maize every day, either as a soup, or made into pancakes called **tortillas**. Before planting maize, farmers prayed to gods such as Tlaloc, who brought rain and made the soil fertile. The picture below shows Tlaloc blessing the maize. He is shown with his young wife, with a digging stick in front of her.

✎ DID YOU KNOW? 🌿

Aztec farmers had to grow about 40 million kilograms of maize each year to feed the people of Tenochtitlan.

Human manure was collected, and spread on the fields as fertilizer to help crops grow, and also keep the city clean.

Tomatoes, squash, beans and flowers grew well on the chinampas. Animals such as turkeys were also raised there.

The chinampas yielded up to seven crops a year.

WHAT DID THE AZTECS EAT?

Maize was the basic food of the Aztecs. **Tortillas** or maize pancakes are still eaten in Mexico today. There were no cattle or sheep, so there were few dairy products, such as milk. Rich people ate some meat, such as duck or turkey. Poor people lived on a healthy diet of maize, beans and vegetables such as tomatoes, avocados and squash.

▲ DRINKING

The picture above shows older people drinking. Only people over the age of thirty were allowed to drink alcohol. However that did not stop younger people from drinking, especially at banquets. Rich people also drank a special non-alcoholic drink made from cocoa beans. We call it chocolate.

▶ FEASTING

Duck, turkey and even dog were served at banquets. One merchant provided 100 turkeys and 40 dogs in a sauce for his guests. Chillies were an essential ingredient at feasts.

◀ CACTUS ALCOHOL

A strong alcoholic drink called **pulque** was made from the sap of a spiky cactus plant called maguey. This sap was also used to make sweet syrup, and the plant fibres were woven to make cloth, ropes and nets.

Squash

Avocados

Sweet potatoes

Duck

Cocoa beans

Tomatoes

Chillies

Turkey

Sweetcorn

▲ PALACE RATIONS

Aztec palaces needed enough food to feed 2,000 people. They needed 20,000 tortillas every day. Ten baskets of tomatoes, 40 baskets of chillies, 100 turkeys, 20 loaves of bread and 140 kilograms of beans were also used every day.

TORTILLAS

450 grams plain flour
1 teaspoon baking powder
1 teaspoon salt
1 tablespoon fat
175 millilitres cold water

Tortillas are quite easy to make. Mix the flour, baking powder and salt together. Now rub in the fat until the mixture looks like breadcrumbs. Add the water and mix to make a dough. Make a dozen balls of dough and roll them out on a surface sprinkled with flour. Grill or fry the tortillas quickly, and add a filling such as cooked beans or cheese.

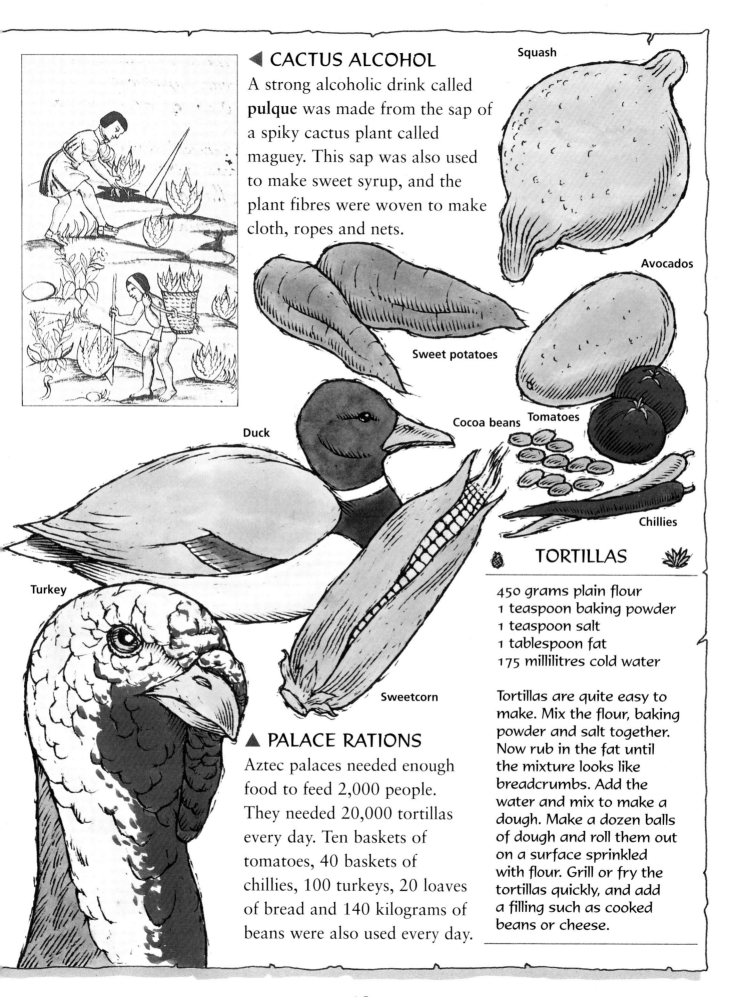

15

WHAT WERE AZTEC FAMILIES LIKE?

Marriage and family life were very important to the Aztecs. Women were respected for having children, just as men were respected for fighting

battles. Ordinary men had one wife, but many noblemen had several wives. People got married at about twenty. They often lived with their parents and grandparents, who gave advice.

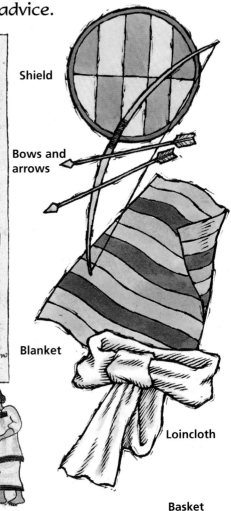

Shield

Bows and arrows

Blanket

Loincloth

Basket

▲ MARRIAGE

Marriages were arranged by parents with the help of a **matchmaker**. When a marriage was arranged, there were several feasts, and presents of maize and cloaks were given. The picture above shows a matchmaker carrying a bride to the groom's house. Here the young couple's clothes were tied together as a symbol of marriage.

FAMILY DUTIES ▼

All family members had duties. Men mainly worked outside the home, as farmers and soldiers for example. Women looked after the household. All girls learned to cook and weave, even in rich households where there were servants. All children learned to be obedient and to respect older people.

▲ NEW BABIES

When a baby was born, relatives arrived with presents and advice. An **astrologer** predicted the child's future, then it was washed and named. Baby boys were given a tiny shield and arrows, while baby girls received a **spindle** and weaving tools.

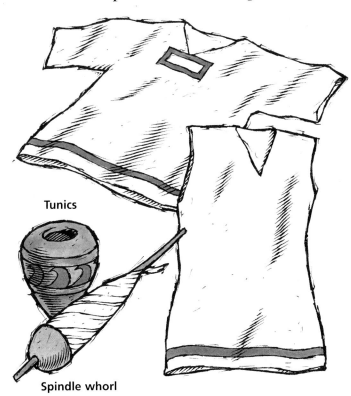

Tunics

Spindle whorl

PREGNANCY

Pregnant women received a lot of advice, some of which was quite sensible.

- Do not lift heavy objects.
- Do not go out at night for fear of spirits.
- Do not look at anything frightening – or anything red.

If a woman died in childbirth she was given great honour.

17

WHAT WERE AZTEC HOUSES LIKE?

The Aztec capital, Tenochtitlan, was built on an island in a shallow lake. The **causeways** that linked the island to the mainland were wide enough to take ten horses. In 1500, Tenochtitlan was larger than any city in Europe, with about 250,000 people. The city had brightly painted palaces and temples.

▶ A BEAUTIFUL CITY

The Spanish were amazed by the beauty of the Aztec capital. One of the visitors wrote: "We saw great towers and temples all built of stone, and rising from the water. Some of our soldiers asked whether the things we saw were but a dream". As well as palaces, Tenochtitlan also had baths, law courts, a zoo and a university.

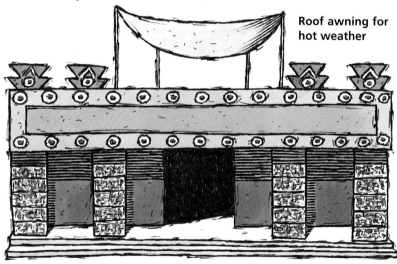

Roof awning for hot weather

Courtyard with pool

◀ HOUSES

Some Aztec houses were made of mud bricks dried in the sun. Most were made of soft stone that was easy to cut into blocks. Ordinary people lived in one-roomed houses with a flat roof that provided more living space. Nobles lived in two-storey houses built around a central courtyard with a pool, and decorated with flowers.

◀ DAILY LIFE

The Aztecs spent a lot of time outdoors, but went to bed at dusk. No one except priests went out at night, for fear of evil spirits. There was good public **sanitation**, and everyone helped to sweep the streets. Indoors, sweeping was girls' work. Here a mother makes her daughter sweep at night, as a punishment.

▶ FURNITURE

Aztec homes had little furniture. There were no beds – people slept on reed mats on the floor. Every home had a **loom** for weaving. Clothing was kept in wooden boxes. Pottery was used to hold drinks and for cooking. These cups were used for **pulque**.

▼ THE FIREPLACE

At the centre of each home was the sacred hearth. Three stones were arranged around the fire, with a flat clay disc on top, which was used for cooking.

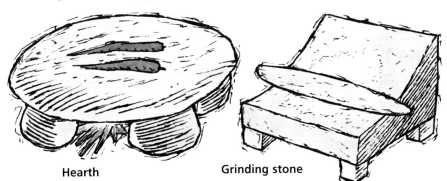

Hearth   **Grinding stone**

CITY FACTS

- The city of Tenochtitlan covered about 12-15 square kilometres.
- Tenochtitlan means "Place of the fruit of the prickly pear cactus". The symbol of the city is shown in the historical drawing on page 18.
- Many homes had a sweat bath in the courtyard. These worked like saunas, and helped people to keep clean and healthy.

DID AZTEC CHILDREN GO TO SCHOOL?

Aztec children started learning skills at an early age. Boys helped to carry water and firewood from the age of four. At six, they were learning to fish and take goods to market. Girls began learning how to spin at the age of four, and how to cook at twelve years old.

▼ WEAVING

This picture shows a mother teaching her daughter to weave.

The **loom** is tied to a wooden post to keep it tight.

▶ SCHOOL WORK

At the age of 15, boys went to one of two schools: either the calmecac or the cuicacalli. The sons of noblemen were taught by priests at the calmecac . Here they learned to read and write, and also had lessons in history, poetry, **astronomy** and religion. The cuicacalli provided fighting training, but all boys learned to fight, and also to farm.

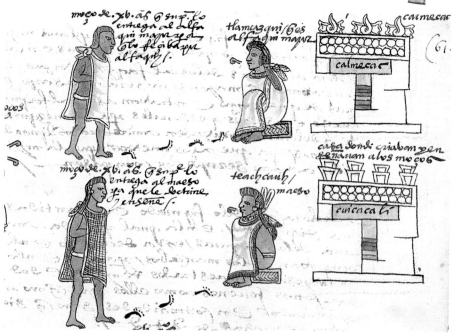

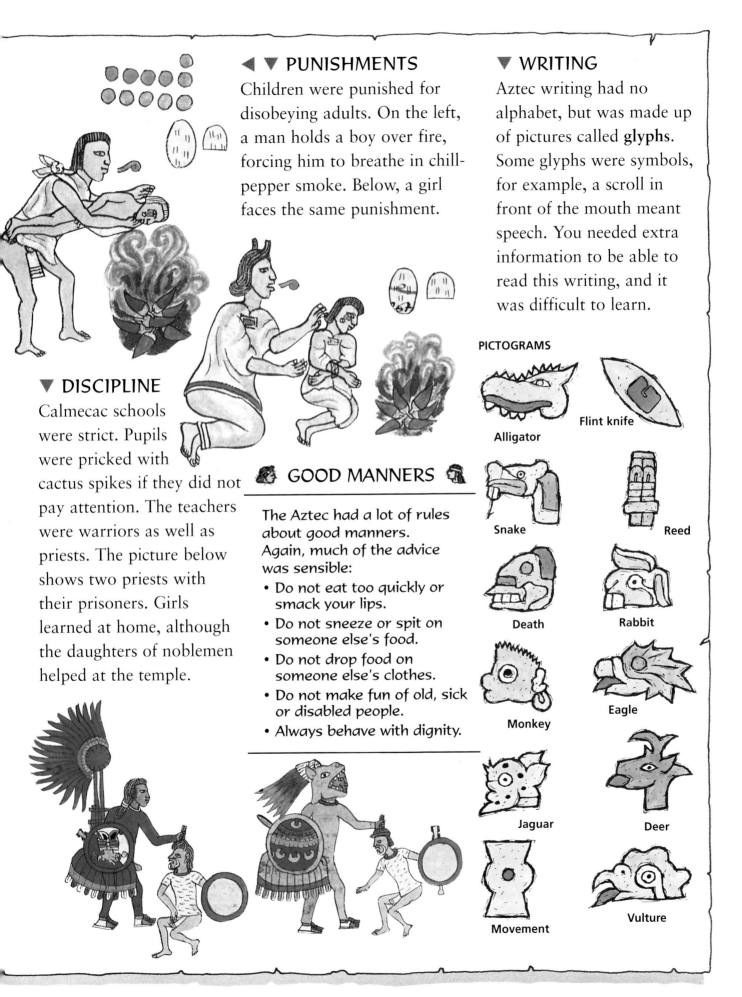

▼ PUNISHMENTS

Children were punished for disobeying adults. On the left, a man holds a boy over fire, forcing him to breathe in chill-pepper smoke. Below, a girl faces the same punishment.

▼ WRITING

Aztec writing had no alphabet, but was made up of pictures called **glyphs**. Some glyphs were symbols, for example, a scroll in front of the mouth meant speech. You needed extra information to be able to read this writing, and it was difficult to learn.

▼ DISCIPLINE

Calmecac schools were strict. Pupils were pricked with cactus spikes if they did not pay attention. The teachers were warriors as well as priests. The picture below shows two priests with their prisoners. Girls learned at home, although the daughters of noblemen helped at the temple.

GOOD MANNERS

The Aztec had a lot of rules about good manners. Again, much of the advice was sensible:

- Do not eat too quickly or smack your lips.
- Do not sneeze or spit on someone else's food.
- Do not drop food on someone else's clothes.
- Do not make fun of old, sick or disabled people.
- Always behave with dignity.

PICTOGRAMS

Alligator

Flint knife

Snake

Reed

Death

Rabbit

Monkey

Eagle

Jaguar

Deer

Movement

Vulture

DID EVERYONE WORK?

Aztec society was based on farmers growing enough food for everyone. But not all Aztecs worked as farmers. Farming methods

were so successful that some people were able to do other work. There were priests, soldiers, merchants, and craftworkers. Some people worked as doctors, **astrologers** and **scribes**.

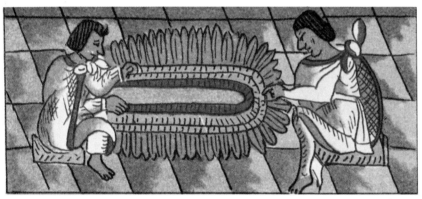

◀ CRAFTWORKERS

Craftworkers were organised into groups called **guilds**. Each guild was based in a particular area. Parents passed on their skills to their children. On the right, a man teaches his son to carve, paint and work with feathers. On the left are featherworkers. Whole families worked in this trade, with women dyeing feathers, men sticking them on the backing, and children making glue.

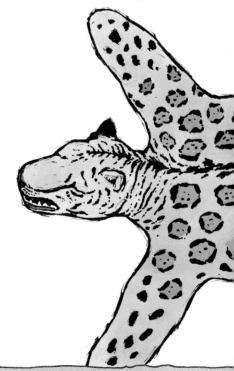

▶ MERCHANTS

Merchants travelled long distances to obtain goods to trade at markets. On the right is Yacatecuhtli, god of merchants. He carries a crossroads with footprints that symbolise long journeys.

◀ METALWORKERS

Metalworkers made jewellery and ornaments. Some objects had working parts, such as birds with flapping wings. Gold and silver were mined in the mountains. They reached the city through trade or as **tribute** – a kind of tax from neighbouring peoples. Each object was unique.

MONEY

Aztecs did not have actual money, but traded different kinds of goods. Cocoa beans were sometimes used as money. Full-time artists who worked in the palaces were paid in squash, beans, chillies, cocoa and cotton before they started. When they finished they were paid two slaves, more cocoa, pottery, salt and clothes.

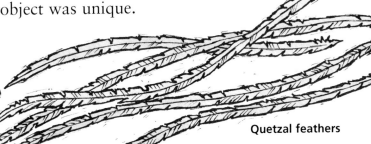

Quetzal feathers

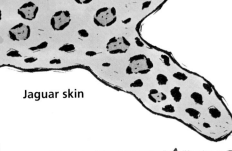

Jaguar skin

HARD WORKERS?

Everyone was meant to work hard, but not everyone did. The **Codices** speak of lazy farmers and careless artists. We also know of cheating merchants who sold mouldy chillies, or tried to pass off cheap cotton as good-quality cloth. There were also fakers, who made false cocoa beans.

WHAT DID PEOPLE DO IN THEIR SPARE TIME?

The Aztecs worked hard, but they had time off for games and festivals. Many festivals were held to honour the gods. Human **sacrifices** were made at these festivals, in the hope that the gods would favour the Aztecs. There were also banquets.

◄ AZTEC BACKGAMMON

Patolli was a popular Aztec game, rather like backgammon. Four cocoa beans painted with white dots were used as dice. Players moved six pebble counters along a board, as shown on the left.

Patolli was a gambling game. Players staked everything they had – clothes, feathers, fields, houses and even their children. Some losers even sold themselves into slavery.

Two-tone drum

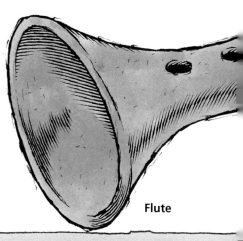

Flute

◀ SACRED BALL GAME

A ball game called **hatchli** or tlatchli was hundreds of years old. It was played in a court up to 60 metres long, with stone rings fixed high on the sides. Teams of players used their hips and knees to bounce the hard rubber ball through a ring. The game had religious meaning, and the losing team was sometimes sacrificed.

▼ MUSIC

Music was played at banquets and festivals. Wind instruments included whistles, flutes and **ocarinas**. Two-tone drums provided a strong beat. Everyone joined in the singing and dancing.

Whistle

POEMS AND PLAYS

Plays, stories and poems like this one expressed hopes and fears:
"Each spring bring us life,
The golden corn
refreshes us,
The pink corn makes
us a necklace.
At least this we know –
The hearts of our friends
are true."

FESTIVALS AND HOLIDAYS

- Aztec festivals included the festival of flowers in July-August, and harvest in September. In October there was a hunting festival. Each festival had human sacrifices.
- People went hunting and fishing both for food and for sport.
- Gardening was popular, but some people preferred just sitting around and gossiping.
- People gave thanks to the gods each morning. They pricked their ears and offered two drops of blood.

Whistle

Ocarina

WHAT DID THE AZTECS WEAR?

The Aztecs had a strict dress code. You could tell a person's **status** from the clothes they wore. It was a crime to wear higher-status clothes. Ordinary people wore coarse cloth made of cactus fibre, while nobles wore more comfortable cotton. Rich people's clothes were more highly decorated.

FINE HEADDRESS ▼

A tall headdress made rulers look more powerful. This one is made of green quetzal feathers and blue cotinga feathers. It may have belonged to Moctezuma.

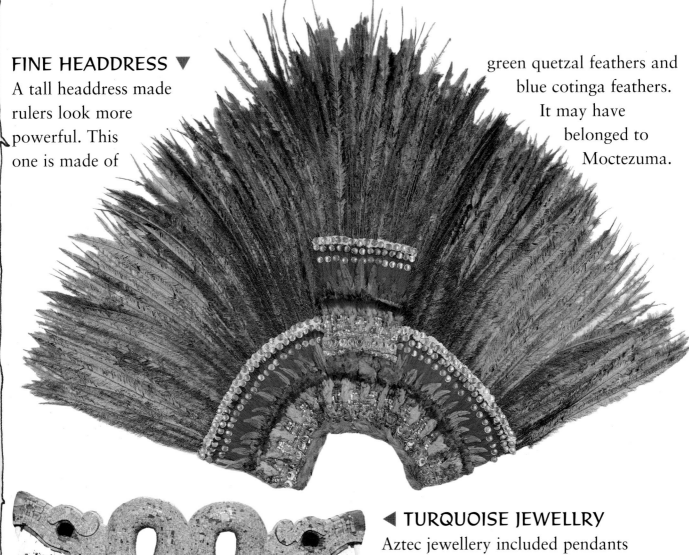

◄ TURQUOISE JEWELLRY

Aztec jewellery included pendants like this one. It is shaped as a double-headed serpent, the symbol of the rain god Tlaloc. The pendant is made of wood covered with turquoise mosaic, and set with red and white shells.

▼ WOMEN'S FASHION

Women wore tunics and long skirts that came below the knee. This statue, of the young wife of the god Tlaloc, shows some women wore their hair loose under a headdress, with plaits at the back. Most married women twisted their plaits around their head so the ends stuck up like horns.

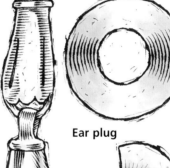

◀ ▼ GOLD AND JADE

Only nobles were allowed to wear jewellery. Both men and women wore gold earrings, and nose- and lip-plugs. A green stone called jade was even more highly prized than gold. Small jade pendants were given to babies as good luck charms.

Pendant

Ear plug

Nose plug

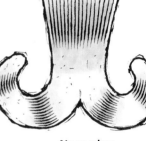

Nose plug

Lip plug

HAIRSTYLES

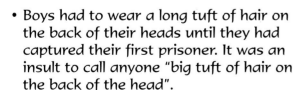

- Boys had to wear a long tuft of hair on the back of their heads until they had captured their first prisoner. It was an insult to call anyone "big tuft of hair on the back of the head".
- Girls washed, combed and oiled their hair.
- Priests did not wash or cut their hair, so it was often full of lice and smelt.

MEN'S CLOTHES ▶

Men wore a loincloth knotted at the front, and a cloak knotted at the shoulder. Only nobles and people with battle-scars on their legs were allowed to wear long cloaks below the knee, as this brave warrior is doing.

WHO DID THE AZTECS WORSHIP?

The Aztecs worshipped many gods and goddesses. From the beginning of time they believed that there had been four previous worlds. These had been destroyed by jaguars, wind, fire and water. The present world would be destroyed by earthquakes. Human **sacrifices** were needed to make the sun rise every day.

◀ EARTH MOTHER

This statue comes from the Great Temple at Tenochtitlan. It shows Coatlicue, the Earth Mother. She is also called "Great Lady of the Serpent Skirt". She stands for the harshness of life, and the serpents on her skirt **represent** poverty. The skull at her belt stands for death.

▼ SMOKING MIRROR

This painting shows Tezcatlipoca or "Smoking Mirror", god of magic, war and death. The Aztecs believed that he was always at war with Quetzalcoatl, the Lord of Life.

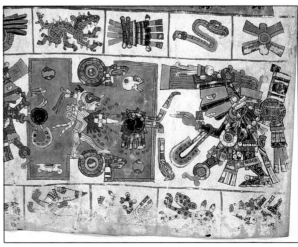

▼ SKULL RACKS

Skull racks stood at every temple. After people were sacrificed, their skulls were put onto poles and left to rot. They believed the world would end without human sacrifice.

▶ GOD OF NEW LIFE

Xipe Totec was god of new life and god of suffering. He is shown wearing a human skin because during his festival, a prisoner was skinned alive. The priest wore the skin to represent new life coming from old.

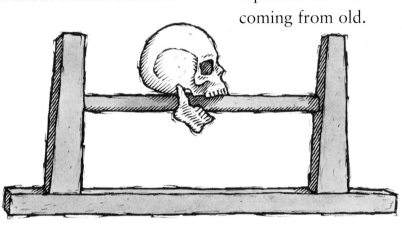

◀ TEMPLES

The Aztecs had many temples. As well as their own gods, they also worshipped the gods of other local peoples. Every home had its own altar. During festivals people went to the temple. Sacrifices were made at the top of a steep staircase so everyone could see.

 GODS

- Aztec gods could be recognised by their different headdresses and colours.
- Xochipilli, Prince of Flowers, was god of the dawn, love, dance and the ball game. He wore flowered sandals and was painted red.
- Huehueteotl, god of fire, was shown as a toothless old man.
- Tloque Nahuaque, the supreme force, was both male and female.

WHAT DID THE AZTECS BELIEVE ABOUT DEATH?

The Aztecs believed in life after death. Warriors, victims of **sacrifices** and women who died in childbirth were given special burial ceremonies. Most people were **cremated**, and went to a gloomy underworld called Mictlan, which they reached after a difficult journey.

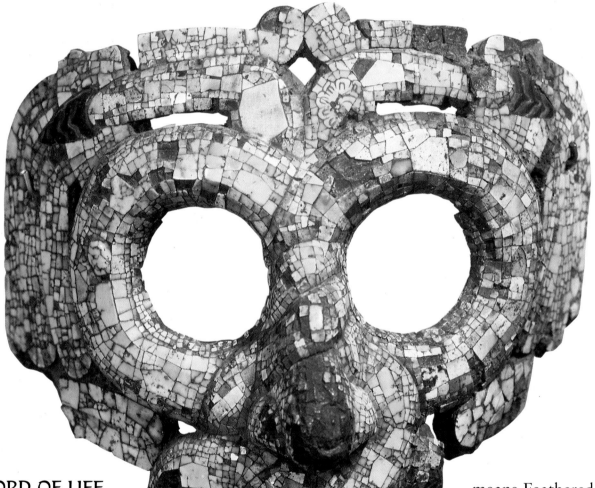

▶ **LORD OF LIFE**
This mask, covered with turquoise, **represents** the god Quetzalcoatl. He was the Lord of Life who created humans. He also brought fertility. His name means Feathered Serpent, and the eyes of the mask are made of serpents. According to legend, Quetzalcoatl sacrificed himself for his people, and became the bringer of life.

▼ SACRIFICIAL KNIFE

Human sacrifices were made with ceremonial knives like this one. It is made of a sharp, hard stone called **obsidian**.

▼ A MERCHANT'S BURIAL

Merchants were seen as fortunate people, who might escape hardship in the Afterlife if properly buried. The picture below shows a merchant's body, which has been carefully wrapped. It is surrounded by possessions.

▶ LORD OF THE DEAD

The journey to Mictlan was long and dangerous. The dead passed through the Wind of Knives, where their flesh was stripped from their bones. Living skeletons like this one feasted and danced at the court of the Lord of the Dead.

Pottery figure of a living skeleton

HUMAN SACRIFICE

- The Aztecs believed that human sacrifice pleased the gods and kept the world going. The gods needed human blood.
- In the usual method of sacrifice, the priest cut out the heart of the victim.

- At the maize festival, a girl's head was cut off. Her blood helped to make sure the harvest was good. No one knew who would be sacrificed.
- Some prisoners were drugged and then skinned alive.

WHO RULED THE AZTECS?

The Aztec world was made up of several **city-states**, each of which was ruled by a Great Speaker. By 1500 Tenochtitlan had become the most important city, and its Great Speaker ruled a large empire. He was chosen from members of the royal family by a group of noblemen.

NOBLES AND COMMONERS ▲

Aztec society was like a pyramid, with the Great Speaker at the top and slaves at the bottom. Below the ruler were the nobles, who traced their families back to the first Aztec ruler. Below the nobles were commoners, who were organised into clans called calpulli. Each calpulli held land which was given to all its members to work. Slaves, who were usually prisoners or criminals, did most of the work on the nobles' lands. A commoner could become a noble if he captured four prisoners alive. Above are three high-ranking soldiers.

▶ GREAT SPEAKERS

The Great Speakers all had special picture-signs for their names. Moctezuma II was shown by a crowned head. Ahuitzotl, was shown by a long-tailed animal. This symbol appears on the carving below.

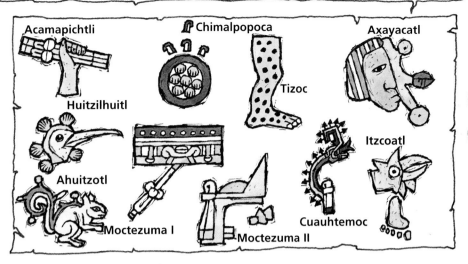

Acamapichtli
Chimalpopoca
Axayacatl
Huitzilhuitl
Tizoc
Ahuitzotl
Itzcoatl
Moctezuma I
Cuauhtemoc
Moctezuma II

◀ DUTIES OF THE RULER

The Great Speaker had great wealth and power. As well as ruler of the Aztecs, he was also commander of the army, chief judge, and head of government. He ruled with the help of an advisor called Snake Woman, who was always a man.

NEW CONQUESTS

The reign of each ruler started with war and conquest. Many prisoners had to be captured and **sacrificed** at the ruler's **coronation**. Temples collapsing in flames, shown on the right, were symbols of conquest. The Aztecs had to keep fighting to make the empire bigger, to support everyone involved in running the empire.

FRIENDS AND FOES

Every city-state had its own laws. Aztec laws were harsh. They were designed to maintain order and society.

Nobles got even harsher punishments than commoners because they were supposed to set a good example.

Judges had to be fair and not take bribes. Lying in court was forbidden and the punishment was death!

WERE THE AZTECS GREAT ARTISTS?

Aztec artists were very skillful. Their skills were a gift from the gods, and were used to honour the gods, so artists did not sign their work. Many people could not read or write, so sculpture, paintings and symbols were used to explain ideas.

◀ GIANT SCULPTURES

Large stone sculptures stood at every temple. Some were over two metres tall. Every god had special symbols and colours, but the colours have faded now. Tlaloc's long teeth made him easy to recognise.

▼ CHACMOOLS

The Toltecs, lived in the valley before the Aztecs, and carved statues called **chacmools**. These stood at the temple entrance. The Aztecs carried on this tradition.

▼ ANIMAL ART

The snake is a common symbol in Aztec art. This animal was linked with the Earth and fertility. The word coatl, meaning snake, appears in the names of several gods. Snakes' heads were carved on the outside of temples. Real snakes were kept in jars lined with feathers.

FEATHERWORKING ▶

Aztec featherwork was so fine it almost looked like painting. Turkey and heron feathers were used along with the bright features of birds such as quetzals, cotingas and parrots. Dull feathers were dyed to make them colourful. The feathers were either glued to a special backing or sewn onto cloth.

COLOURS

Aztec painters used natural colours and did not mix them.
Red – from cochineal, made from crushed insects.
Green – made from vegetable dye.
Blue – came from chalk, dyed with flowers.
Yellow – came from a soil called ochre.
Purple – made from the crushed shells of sea snails.

▶ PAINTERS

Books, or **Codices**, were known as thought paintings. They were made of long strips of deerskin. They could be up to six metres long, with paintings on both sides. The artists who made them were called "putters-down of thoughts" or tlacuilo.

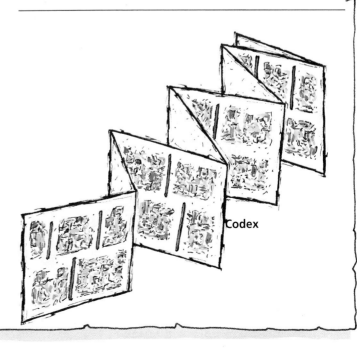

Codex

DID THE AZTECS USE TECHNOLOGY?

The Aztecs were master-builders and clever doctors. **Astronomers** studied the stars and invented calendars. But Aztec society was based on farming, so Aztecs were not very interested in technology. They had no wheeled vehicles and no need for more effective weapons as war was a **ritual** in honour of the gods.

CALENDAR STONE ▼

This carved calendar stone shows the sun god in the centre, surrounded by pictures of the end of the world. The days of the year are marked on the outer ring. Aztec priests used this stone to predict **eclipses** of the sun.

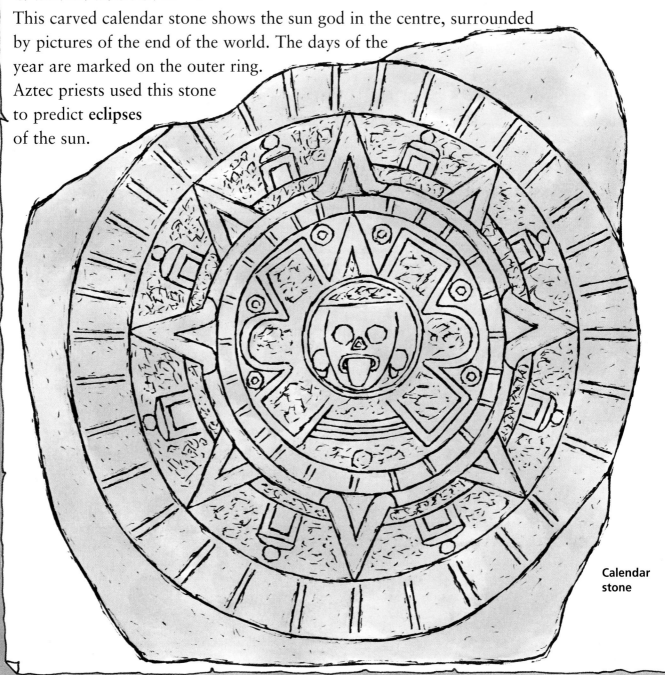

Calendar stone

 ## ASTRONOMY

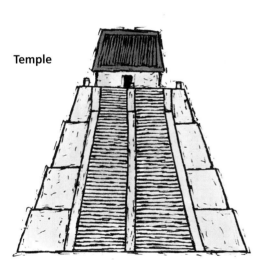

Temple

- The Aztecs used three calendars. The sacred calendar had 260 days with 20 months of 13 days each.
- The farming or **solar** year contained 365 days like our year. The farming year was divided into 18 months with 20 days each. The five spare days were unlucky.
- The third calendar was linked to the **orbit** of the planet Venus. It had 584 days.
- Aztec astronomers **calculated** the orbits of the planets Mars and Venus by watching the night sky.

MEDICINE ▼▲

Aztec doctors used herbs to cure and prevent illness. Doctors could be men or women, as you can see in the pictures. They understood a lot about the human body because war and **sacrifices** provided plenty of bodies to practise on!

DID THE AZTECS TRAVEL?

The Aztecs started out as a travelling people who wandered from place to place. But once they reached the valley, they preferred to stay there. By 1500, the only people who travelled were merchants and warriors, searching for new lands to conquer. A noble wrote: "We must continue to march onwards".

▲ WATER TRAVEL
Dugout canoes like the one on page 39 were used to transport goods by water. These canoes were made from a single tree trunk. The larger sea canoe shown above is carrying American Indians and Spaniards on their way to fight the Aztecs.

PORTERS ▶
Most travellers went on foot. People carried their goods on their backs because there were no carts or horses. A strap around the forehead helped to support the load. A network of tracks linked different parts of the empire. Porters would jog along these tracks, carrying up to 40 kilograms. This carving shows the god Quetzalcoatl as a porter.

MERCHANT TRAVELLERS
Merchants travelled far and wide to fetch goods to trade at markets. These long journeys could be dangerous, since the traders could be ambushed and robbed. However by 1500, Aztec merchants had become rich and powerful.

They also acted as spies, bringing information back to the government. They were the first to bring news of strangers arriving from overseas in "winged birds". These were the Spanish **galleons** – the Aztecs had never seen sailing ships before.

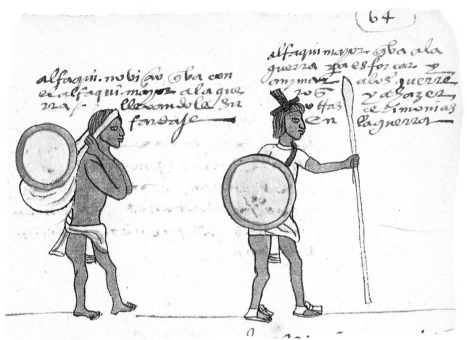

◀ SOLDIERS

This painting shows a young priest going off to war. A porter follows with his kit. Soldiers went on long journeys to conquer new peoples, who then had to send **tributes** back to the empire. These goods were used to feed and clothe the Aztecs. Conquered peoples also provided victims for **sacrifice**.

▼ TREASURE

This ceremonial shield shows the long-tailed animal that **represents** the ruler Ahuitzotl. Made of feathers and outlined with gold, it was a valuable treasure. Objects like this made the Spanish want more treasure, and led them to fight and conquer the Aztecs.

MARKETS

Markets were important places in every town. They were where people met to buy goods and also exchange gossip. Every market sold local produce and also goods brought from far and wide. People arrived from the countryside with copper axe-blades or jade beads to trade. Even Europeans who had visited cities such as Rome had never seen such big and bustling markets.

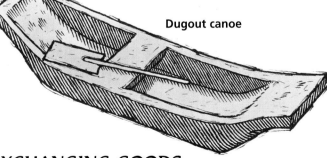

Dugout canoe

EXCHANGING GOODS

Cocoa beans, cotton cloaks and copper bells could all be exchanged as money. Everything had a value. One strip of pine-bark could be swapped for one egg and two cocoa beans.

DID THE AZTECS HAVE AN ARMY?

The Aztec state could not survive without war. Wars with neighbouring peoples provided more land, people and resources for the ever-growing population. There was no professional army, but there were professional army officers. Soldiers were ordinary people, because every boy was trained to fight.

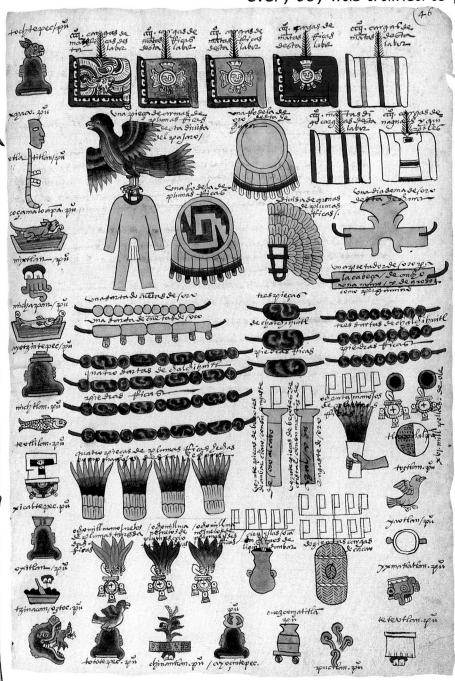

◄ TRIBUTE

The Aztec state could not survive on its own. It needed outside help. This came in the form of **tributes** – enforced gifts from conquered peoples. Defeated enemies had to pay a yearly tribute of food and luxury goods, a kind of tax. This page from a **Codex** shows the tributes that were paid.

In a year, one coastal province had to send nearly 10,000 cloaks, 2,000 tunics, a gold shield, gold and jade necklaces, 40 lip-plugs, 80 bunches of quetzal feathers, 16,000 rubber balls, and 20 sacks of cocoa.

If a region refused to pay, it was punished. The tribute was made more difficult. For example, the Aztecs asked for live snakes and double-size cloaks.

SACRIFICE ▶

Ritual battles called "wars of the flowers" were fought for religious reasons. Men were needed for **sacrifice** – and sacrifice made sure that the sun continued to rise, and crops continued to flourish. It was thought an honour to be sacrificed. Captured soldiers became part of their **captor's** family until it was time for them to die.

SPIES

Merchants who knew the area were disguised as peasants and spied on enemy territory. There were even reports of spies tunnelling under enemy camps to overhear information.

Clubs

Spears

▲ WEAPONS

Aztec weapons included deadly flint-bladed clubs and spears tipped with sharp **obsidian** blades. Throwing sticks were used to make spears travel further. A round shield with a long fringe protected soldiers from enemy attack.

▼ TAKING PRISONERS

The costume of this warrior shows he has taken many prisoners already.

 ## CANNIBALISM

The Aztecs ate human flesh. This practice is called cannibalism.

The arms and legs of victims were cut off, stewed and eaten by the captor's relatives. It was thought rude to eat your own prisoners, but you could eat someone else's.

The Aztecs fed the rest of the body to animals in the zoo.

WHAT HAPPENED TO THE AZTECS?

While the Aztecs were expanding their empire, so were European countries. In the early 1500s, the Spanish crossed the Atlantic Ocean in search of land and gold. The Aztecs were very religious. They thought that the Spanish with their horses and guns resembled gods.

▲ ▶ SPANISH INVASION

In 1519, Hernan Cortes landed on the Mexican coast with a force of 350 soldiers. The Spanish made friends with a people called the Tlaxcalans, enemies of the Aztecs. Together they marched on to Tenochtitlan. The Spanish entered the city and were greeted by the Aztec leader, Moctezuma.

CONQUEST AND DESTRUCTION

The Spanish tried to take over the city but the Aztecs rebelled, killing many Spanish soldiers. Moctezuma was killed, probably by the Spanish. Cortes escaped. He returned in 1521 and conquered Tenochtitlan. The Spanish destroyed the city and the temple.

END OF AN EMPIRE

Tenochtitlan was flattened. The Great Temple was destroyed and a Christian cathedral was built. Spanish missionaries converted the local people to Christianity.

Aztec lands became a Spanish colony. Gold and treasure was sent across the sea to Spain.

The Spanish killed many Aztecs. Thousands more died of diseases brought by the Spanish. In just 50 years, the Aztec population fell from over 12 million to about 1 million.

▲ ANCIENT REMAINS

Mexico City, the capital of Mexico, now stands on the site of Tenochtitlan. These statues were found in the ruins of the Great Temple.

GLOSSARY

AD The abbreviation of 'Anno Domini' used to show that a date is of the Christian era, which started with the birth of Christ.

ARCHAEOLOGIST A person who explores the past civilisations by digging up their remains.

ASTROLOGER A person who uses the stars to predict the future.

ASTRONOMY The scientific study of the stars and planets.

CALCULATE To work out.

CAPTOR Someone who captures someone or something.

CAUSEWAY A bridge, usually made of earth.

CHACMOOL A statue used to hold the blood of sacrificial victims.

CHINAMPAS The "floating gardens" of the Aztecs.

CITY-STATE An independent state based on a city.

CODICES The picture books of the Aztecs. One book is called a Codex.

CORONATION When a new ruler is crowned.

CREMATE When someone's body is burned rather than being buried.

ECLIPSE When the Moon comes between the Sun and the Earth, so the Sun's light is blocked.

GALLEON An old-time sailing ship.

GLYPH A picture symbol, used in Aztec writing.

GUILD An organisation of workers.

HATCHLI The sacred ball game of the Aztecs, also called tlatchli.

LOOM A machine for weaving.

MATCHMAKER Someone who arranges marriages.

OBSIDIAN A glassy volcanic stone.

OCARINA A type of wind instrument.

ORBIT When a planet circles the sun, or the Moon circles the Earth.

PATOLLI An Aztec board game, similar to backgammon.

PULQUE An alcoholic drink made from the sap of the maguey cactus.

REPRESENT To stand for something.

RITUAL A ceremony, or something that is carried out in a formal way.

SACRIFICES Valuable offerings made to please a god. Some sacrifices involved the killing of a person or an animal.

SANITATION Public hygiene.

SCRIBE A professional writer.

SOLAR Of or belonging to the sun.

SPINDLE A spinning tool.

STATUS A person's position in society.

TORTILLA A maize pancake.

TRIBUTE An enforced gift, a kind of tax.

INDEX